The Lost Fishhook

Kath Lock

Illustrated by Xiangyi Mo and Jingwen Wang

Based on a story from Japan

P9-BUI-946

1998 Barrie Publishing Pty Limited
The Lost Fishhook
Text copyright © Kath Lock
Illustrations copyright © Xiangyi Mo and Jingwen Wang

Momentum program © Barrie Publishing Pty Limited

Published by Troll Communications L.L.C.
Reprinted by arrangement with Barrie Publishing Pty Limited,
Suite 513, 89 High Street, Kew, Australia, 3101

ISBN 0 8167 5020 3

Printed in Singapore by PH Productions Pte Ltd
10 9 8 7 6 5 4 3 2 1

Contents

Chapter One

The Two Brothers

Long, long ago in Japan there were two brothers.
The elder brother was the Prince of the Sea, and
the younger brother was the Prince of the
Mountains. Each of them was skilled at hunting in
his own domain.

It seemed no effort for the Prince of the Sea to
cast his line or his nets, return with an enormous
catch, and be praised. When the Prince of the
Mountains went into the forest, his swift arrows
flew straight and found their mark. When he
returned, he brought meat for the villagers, and he
too was praised.

There came a time when there were great storms, and the Prince of the Sea was no longer able to make good catches. He soon became restless and envious of his brother, who was still able to bring food from the mountains.

"You've been hunting in the mountains since we were children," he said to his brother one day. "How would you like to try your hand at fishing? There is a tremendous challenge in catching what you cannot see. Why don't we change places for a while?"

The younger brother was not deceived, but he knew his brother was unhappy, so he agreed.

At the end of the first day, both brothers returned empty-handed. The Prince of the Sea was angrier than ever, for he had felt sure that hunting would be easier than fishing.

Even worse, his brother had lost his favorite fishing hook.

No matter what the Prince of the Mountains did, he could not placate his brother. He had metal workers make fishhooks that were delicate and fishhooks that were strong. None pleased his brother. He insisted that only the lost fishhook would return his skill at fishing.

Chapter Two

The Journey

The Prince of the Mountains spent many days at the beach searching hopelessly for the lost hook. One day he found a bird trapped in a snare, struggling to get free. The Prince took pity on the bird and carefully opened the trap. As soon as the bird was free, it changed into an old man.

"Why do you wander along this beach every day, searching through the sand?" asked the old man.

"I've lost my brother's favorite fishhook, and he seems determined to torment me until it is found," replied the Prince.

"Don't worry," said the old man, "I can help you. First, you must go to the bottom of the sea and find the Sea King's palace. Then, you must ask the Sea King whether he knows where the lost fishhook can be found. You will be safe, for I shall take care of you."

So the Prince of the Mountains set off on his journey to the bottom of the sea, and just as the old man had foretold, he was kept from drowning and saw many wondrous sights. The deeper he went, the more beautiful were the surroundings, until suddenly he saw what could only be the palace of the Sea King.

The garden was filled with shells, sea-flowers, and such exotic-looking fish that the Prince of the Mountains could only stand and stare.

As the Prince gazed in wonder at the sea garden, he saw a lovely maiden sitting on a rock. When she saw him she disappeared and soon returned with her father, the Sea King.

"Who are you? Where do you come from and why are you here in my kingdom?" the Sea King asked.

"Your Majesty, I am the Prince of the Mountains, and I am descended from the great God of the Sky. I was sent to your kingdom to find my brother's fishhook. He is Prince of the Sea and has made my life miserable since I lost it. I cannot return to my home until it is found."

The Sea King invited the Prince of the Mountains to stay at the palace until the fishhook was found.

Chapter Three

The Palace of the Sea King

Now it happened that the Prince of the Mountains found life at the palace of the Sea King so pleasant that he forgot all about the fishhook. Each day he walked in the palace gardens with the Princess. He told her of the great beauty of the animals and birds of the forest in the mountains where he hunted. The Princess showed him the splendor of the sea, and it was only a short time before the two were in love. The Sea King was delighted, for he had grown to love the Prince as a son, and a grand wedding was prepared.

For three years the Prince of the Mountains lived happily in the palace of the Sea King with his beautiful bride. One day, when he was telling her about his homeland, he felt a great yearning to return home. Then he remembered his brother's fishhook.

When the Sea King heard of his son-in-law's longing for home, he called all the fishes of the sea together and asked if they had seen the special hook that belonged to the Prince of the Sea. None had seen it. But one old fish complained of having had a sore mouth for a very long time. When the Sea King examined her, sure enough, there inside her mouth was the hook that belonged to the Prince of the Sea.

"I know that you must return to your homeland," the Sea King said to his son-in-law, "but when you do, you must immediately prepare a palace worthy of my daughter. It must be near the sea, and its roof must be made of the wings of beautiful cormorants. In one month my daughter will come to you. The palace must be finished. If she is happy there, you will find that creatures will live in harmony in the two kingdoms of the Land and the Sea. Your brother might not be pleased to see you, so take this magic tool with you. It has great power over the tides. You have only to ask, and it will bring in a flood tide or cause an ebb tide whenever you wish."

The Prince of the Mountains thanked the Sea King and promised that he would immediately build such a palace for his bride. He returned to his homeland and gave the fishhook to his brother. Just as the Sea King had predicted, his brother was not pleased. He had believed that the Prince of the Mountains would never return, and had enjoyed being able to rule over the whole kingdom. When taunts and harsh words failed to anger his brother, the Prince of the Sea became violent and did all that he could to harm his brother.

Finally, in order to save himself from his brother's sword, the Prince of the Mountains called on the magic tool of the sea to bring a flood tide. The Prince of the Sea was taken away by the terrible swirling waters.

The Prince of the Mountains grieved for his brother. Many days had now passed since he had sworn to keep his promise to the Sea King. He knew that he must hurry.

Chapter Four

The Promise

In deep sorrow, he began to build a palace that
would be fitting for his bride and their child who
was soon to be born.

Each morning he said prayers for his brother's
soul, then he set to work on the palace. Day and
night he worked at laying the cormorants' wings
on the palace roof, for he felt that this special task
should be done only by him. It was not long
before the palace was nearly finished. There were
just a few more cormorants' wings to be laid on
the roof.

That night, as the sun sank into the sea, the Sea King's daughter emerged from the sea astride a giant turtle.

"My husband," she said. "You have broken your promise to my father. You delayed building the palace while fighting with your brother. Creatures of the two kingdoms will not live in harmony. I can stay with you for only one year after our child is born. But my father has promised that if we are happy during that time, when he dies I will be free to live with you and our child."

True to her word, one year after their son was born, the Sea King's daughter sat astride the giant turtle and disappeared into the sea.

The Prince of the Mountains lived in the palace by the sea with his son who learned to catch fish, just as his uncle had done.

The Prince of the Mountains grieved for his brother whose love had been spoiled by envy, and he and his son longed for the day when the Princess would return.